THE HUMAN NATURE
OF A UNIVERSITY

THE
HUMAN NATURE
OF A
UNIVERSITY

BY ROBERT F. GOHEEN

PRINCETON, NEW JERSEY

PRINCETON UNIVERSITY PRESS

1969

Library of Congress Card Number: 72-93473
Standard Book Number: 691-09348-2

This book has been composed in Linotype Monticello

Printed in the United States of America
by Princeton University Press

TO MY FAMILY

FOREWORD

I SHOULD LIKE to express my thanks to William McCleery, who took a foot-high collection of speeches and reports and other papers written by me during twelve years as President of Princeton and distilled from it this little book.

The words are mine but the "plot," the arrangement into what I hope the reader will find an agreeable and unified whole, is his. Each chapter is made up of excerpts—sometimes several paragraphs, sometimes a few lines—from as many as ten different documents.

Thus, for better or worse, the reader gets in one thin volume a sampling not of what I said last month or last year but of what I have been saying for the last dozen years. Moreover, thanks to his skillful blending of the excerpts, what might have been a series of snapshots of a university president's mind at work emerges, instead, for better or worse, as a portrait; one that I, at least, recognize.

Whatever the merits of the materials, Mr. McCleery seems to me to have done a fine job of organizing them; no more than one would expect from the Editor of *University: A Princeton Quarterly*.　　　ROBERT F. GOHEEN

NASSAU HALL
PRINCETON UNIVERSITY

CONTENTS

1

OUT OF TENSIONS, PROGRESS

UNIVERSITIES are increasingly in the news today, not only because of student unrest and enlarging campus populations, but also because the role of universities as centers of teaching and research has been getting more pervasive and more critical in myriad aspects of our national life. In Washington and in the state capitals, in city offices, on farms, and in homes, people find reason to give heed to the once-sequestered halls of higher learning.

Ironically, as more attention is paid and more people are involved, there seems to be less understanding of what a university *is*, other than simply a training ground. Everyone apparently has a pretty clear idea of what a hospital is for and how it works, or a law court, or a school; but despite the torrents of printed words about universities these days, there seems to me to be a vast amount of misunderstanding about them. And along with this misunderstanding, there is questioning—often with the wrong questions being asked—and there is distrust.

The purpose of this volume is to try to shed some light on certain essential aspects of the university, generically viewed. The objective is not to set down guidelines for the handling of protesting students, or for dealing with disaffected faculty members, or troublesome trustees, or even political figures who nowadays, increasingly, show an inclination to tell the university how to conduct its affairs. I would hope, though, that light shed on the university's basic nature might help to illuminate these and other problem areas.

In many ways, a university is a loose and peculiar association of persons, assembled for the pursuit of knowledge and understanding. Misunderstanding grows at least in part out of the tendency so many of us have to see others only as stereotypes—even in a day of instant and wide communications. Thus we hear pronouncements about

· 4 ·

university faculties as if they walked in lock-step and could be uniformly labeled. It has been my observation that if you gather a hundred professors together, you have a hundred individualists. Professors may kick—often do—but seldom with unisoned precision.

Another stereotype is applied to college students—as if over six million young men and women engaged in higher education in this country could be categorized simply! I have known a good many of them and I see few signs of a common stamp.

Then there is the alumnus. If anyone harbors the notion that the alumni of any university form a solid, homogenized phalanx of nostalgic, reactionary "old grads," let him read my mail for a week. As for trustees, I can only say that if those of my own university are a fair example, they are certainly no clutch of corporate tycoons, as the stereotype would have them. From physicians to scientists, to clergymen, to lawyers, to publishers, to educators—as well as to bankers and businessmen—the trustees I have seen at Princeton and elsewhere tend to be a cross-section of the leadership in American life. As such, they rarely agree unanimously—as I well know. What they do have in common is considerable experience beyond the university and a willingness to give to her generously of their time and effort, without reward and with little recognition.*

As the constituent groups within a university embrace human differences and individualities, so do universities themselves vary widely—in the base of their support, in the range of their activities, and in the way they are organized. From their beginnings in the western world, the universities have persistently resisted pressures to uniformity.

In this country, some are public, some are private, some are a bit of both; some are large, some small; some are church-related, some not; some are confined to one campus, some spread out to many. Universities also differ in the range of their efforts. Some extend themselves widely in programs of direct service for community and state; others tend to stick closely to the traditional business of instruction and scholarship.

Finally, universities are variously organized.

*In a move that both evidenced its present flexibility and promised even greater flexibility in the future, Princeton's Board of Trustees voted in 1969 to provide for the election each spring of a Trustee from the graduating class to serve a 4-year term. Election will be by the junior and senior classes and alumni from the two most recent graduating classes.

One can point to the oligarchic self-governance en-
joyed by the professors in European universities,
or to monarchical presidencies that appeared in
certain late nineteenth-century American institutions, or to the many forms of academic organization to be found on today's campuses—none quite
like the other. Whether one sees the presidency or
the faculty as weak or strong, the governing board
as involved or remote, the decision-making as
more, or less, democratically based—seems to depend mainly upon what institution one is looking
at and at what time.

Today it is clear that there is a marked desire
among many students and many faculty members
to have an effective role in the direction of their
universities. And what is more important, they
seem willing—in principle, at least—to devote
time and effort to it. This was not always so, and
may not be again. As long as faculty and students
are inclined to effective participation, it is in everyone's best interest, I believe, to draw on what they
can contribute. For when decisions are discussed
widely and hammered out jointly among the principal parties of interest, they tend to be sounder
institutional decisions, and the additional time and
effort required to achieve them that way is usu-

ally justified by the wider, readier acceptance they are likely to find.

None of this is to suggest that a university can be run on the principle of one man, one vote. As I shall say repeatedly in this volume, the university's main objective is the advancement of learning and of thought—not its own governance or any other activity. It is not a political entity and not intended to be one. Nevertheless, in my view, if the procedures for student as well as faculty participation are soundly conceived, if responsibility is seriously assumed, and if everyone concerned will work together for the common good with forebearance and mutual respect, the power and authority of the university can be widely and effectively shared.

Yet in this as in most matters, universities may differ greatly. Why should they not?

But if universities are first of all associations of human beings, diverse and variously organized, they nevertheless have significant things in common. All are basically concerned with the advancement of learning. All seek to carry on their proper work in an atmosphere of freedom: freedom to pursue the truth wherever it leads, and *to talk about it*. All are optimistic enterprises, presupposing that man's lot on earth may be improved, albeit slowly, bit by bit. They share, besides, many of the attributes of the human creature. Thus, they are sites of both reason and emotion. They are complex, changeable, but also resistant to change. At their best, they are laudable; at their worst, disappointing; most of the time, both of these at once.

Such is the nature of a university—its human nature. I once saw an abandoned college campus. The broken windows, crumbling brick, cobwebs, and caved-in roofs expressed more eloquently than many words the simple truth that an educational institution does not essentially consist of walls and ivy, but of the human beings who make it up. And just as that which most distinguishes human from other vocal and gregarious forms of life is man's capacity for reasoned thought, so, I submit, a basic commitment to the life if the mind most properly marks the university. It does not seek victories; it does not work for profits; its production is not measurable. Its truest goals are not precise targets, but high ideals—the enrichment of the minds and lives of its students, the advancement of knowledge, the increase of understanding among men, and the unending search for truth.

Obviously, in this imperfect world the loftiness and rightness of a university's aims do not guarantee harmony or insure against disintegration. Much depends upon a subtle, hard-to-define set of human relationships within it, organic filaments of mutual trust and at least minimal friendliness. These are easily broken. When emotion gets astride of reason, when invective displaces argument, when suspicion erodes trust, then the filaments may snap and the university may fall into pieces—into hostile cliques. Or, disturbed by too much discord on campus, outsiders may invite themselves in to "straighten things out"—with results that can only be injurious.

I do not suggest for a moment that there should be no disagreements, no strong feelings, no righteous indignation. Teaching and research do not preclude passion or emotion. On the contrary, scholarly inquiry is often prompted by passion, and scholarly research often helps to clarify men's deepest convictions and make them effective. At the same time, thoughtful examination and reasoned argument must be defended in the university against all who would substitute force and coercive types of protest, or else the university loses its prime function. There may be causes worth shattering a campus for, but when it happens, a very high price is paid.

Like a human being, a university can suffer bruises, be pushed around and temporarily damaged, while yet preserving its basic strength and capacities. Like a human being, it can learn from experience and is adaptable—more adaptable than some would have us believe. But like a human being also, it can suffer irreparable wounds. It can be crippled or even destroyed when attacks are pressed too far against its fundamental nature, which is to be a site and stimulus for the free-ranging, uninhibited, judicious, impartial action of the mind.

As a one-time classicist I am naturally inclined in viewing the university to take my starting point in the distant past. Frequently in recent years my thoughts have been drawn back there—in particular to two of the pre-Socratic philosophers, both men of the early fifth century before Christ.

One was Parmenides of Elea in southern Italy. Perhaps because conditions in the western Greek world of his time were relatively stable, but for other reasons too, Parmenides centered his attention on the permanence of things—or, better, the permanence within things. He banished, as matters of illusion and unsteady opinion (*doksa*), the flux and uncertainties of experience, the transitoriness of events. Against them he set a vision of the real as something without beginning or end, single, constant, motionless, final, complete. All the diversity of nature and of history exist, he said, only "in name"; reason leads us not to them, but to a steady, unchanging world order.

At the other extremity of the Greek world, where the westward thrust of the Persian Empire was being felt, a slightly older contemporary of Parmenides was meantime expounding a very different view of the world and of life. He was Heraclitus of Ephesus. For him movement, tension, and strain were fundamental; "everything comes about by strife and necessity"; "all is flux, nothing is stationary"; the universe is an unending conflict of opposites.

Heraclitus' favorite images were the bow and the lyre. The tension of the bow, the strain put on its opposite ends, gives the arrow force to carry firmly to a mark. In the playing of a lyre, harmony results only where there is contrast—when there is interplay among tones at variance with one another.

Need we ask ourselves which of these men speaks to us today in terms that strike home? Surely it is Heraclitus. A large array of compelling and competing demands bears on every American university to force historic choices. Almost

everywhere we look we encounter forces making for change and strain, and this is no less true in the supposedly tranquil halls of higher learning than in the multitudinous, shifting, shrinking world of human affairs. For the American university of today is very much a part of these affairs both at home and abroad, and increasingly it is subject to heightened and to spreading calls for service—and for change—from the society and the world of which it is a part.

In some this situation evokes dismay; and in most of us no doubt the wish for a calm, stable ordering of things runs strongly. Nevertheless, what we should see plainly is that, within the strains and tensions that confront and involve us, there lies the hope of progress, with great potential benefits to the nation and to mankind. Indeed, as they bend their efforts to respond with vigor and with purpose, our institutions of higher education are likely, I believe, to drive to higher levels of beneficial accomplishment than ever before.

In the pages that follow I shall talk of the modern university in terms of some of the internal tensions that give it dynamism, using the word "tension" in a Heraclitean sense: meaning a cross-pull not of a good thing against an evil thing but, most often, between competing goods.

The tensions dealt with here are only a few of those that exist. I have chosen them because they are the ones I have felt most keenly myself and about which I hope I may have something generally applicable to say. I have omitted some important ones, such as *University & Community*, because, although I have had experience with them, I do not feel that such expertise as I may have gained is exportable. (Universities and their communities vary too widely for generalizations on that subject to be very helpful.) Others such as *Age & Youth* or *Faculty & Students* I have omitted because they are too large to be dealt with profitably in a small book. *Science & the Humanities*—"the two cultures"—has already had at least an adequate airing. *Quantity & Quality*—the pull toward improved education and the counter-pull toward making education available to many more students—is surely one of the most wrenching tensions of our time. This entire book bears upon that one by suggesting—under each of the tensions—what the word "quality" means in higher education.

The book contains, I fear, inevitably, a certain amount of restatement and overlapping, since some principles apply to more than one tension. And some of what I have said under *Conservation*

& Innovation might, for example, have gone under *Detachment & Involvement*—which might instead have been called *The Long View & Relevance*. No claim is made for perfection in the packaging. Nor do I claim to have shed all possible light on the few tensions about which I have chosen to write. I offer this book primarily as *a way of looking at* the university, and at other human institutions: at ourselves, for that matter, though Dr. Freud is well ahead of me in suggesting that human beings who refuse or fail to recognize and deal with their inner conflicts may lose requisite balance and direction, and become ineffectual.

Insofar as its nature is human, the university seems to me to have that same unhappy option.

2

DETACHMENT &
INVOLVEMENT

FEW OF THE TENSIONS facing universities today are new ones. What *is* new is the intensity of the pressures they exert. An example is the cross-pull between the university's need to be detached from the world's turmoil and immediate demands, in order to concentrate on developing manpower and ideas for the future; and at the other end of the bow, the university's need to become involved, to be "relevant," to contribute what it can (and this can be a great deal) to the solution of immediate problems. This cross-pull is greater today than ever before because our society has an unprecedented number of complex immediate problems; and yet anyone with imagination can see both that their roots run deep and that today's problems are simple compared to tomorrow's.

Clearly, most choices between the university's detachment and its involvement in immediate problems have to be made on a case-by-case basis. What I have to say on the point is so general, so elementary, that I hesitate to express it. I do so only because I have found in my years as a university president that one is helped in making even the most complex decisions by referring back to basic principles.

Let me begin, then, with a reminder that there is an activity of the human mind essential to education—to research and instruction and learning—but one often slighted in the urgencies of the hour. I mean careful, dispassionate, reflective thought. To encourage and nurture this private activity is a vital part of any university's business. Indeed, when you strip off everything else, the university is, quintessentially, a center for thought. It is more than a training ground for future leaders; it is more than a headquarters of scholarship and research. Its success in those roles depends finally on this less visible role, namely the creating and preserving of a climate of thought and reflection.

The best minds of our nation and of the western

world are busy indeed these days. The results are seen most spectacularly in the natural sciences, but there is plenty of action in every field. On the byways as well as the highways of learning all across the country, teachers and students are occupied as never before. The Jeffersonian belief in the importance of education for all in a democratic society now goes unchallenged, and America's schools and colleges march on under a flag of faith in a better future through education.

All of which is for the good.

But we need to make certain that in all this bustle and stir something precious is not crowded out. I mean that rare thing, freeborn, untrammeled, individual thought: the kind of thinking that may go contrary to the accepted, that wants to examine—and re-examine—every premise. Such unconstrained, unobstructed thinking and imagining is always in danger precisely because it makes people uncomfortable. Let me quote William H. Whyte, writing in *Fortune* of "The New Illiteracy":

> Every great advance has come out, and always will, because someone was frustrated by the status quo; because someone exercised the skepticism, the questioning and the kind of curiosity which, to borrow a phrase, blows the lid off everything. . . .

What is our democracy but a testament of faith in the individual? Faith not only in our fellow laymen, but faith in our own inner resources, in man's own ability to create and to dream. The new illiteracy would have us suppose that the whole is greater than the sum of the parts, that the system itself has a wisdom beyond the reach of ordinary mortals. But this is not so. The individual can be greater than the group and his own imaginings worth a thousand graphs and studies.

Now, the university is one of few places where the individual can be greater than the group, and his imaginings given free play. By the "individual" I mean not only the faculty member but the student too. The university is a place where, if teaching is sound and alive, students learn to do their own thinking, their own reflecting.

Someone once said that if you subjected university people to the most carefully controlled conditions, under the most meticulous administrative oversight, they would still end up doing and thinking just about as they pleased. And this is as it should be. For even as an exaggeration, the observation points toward the essential nature of a university: a place where people are assembled to press the search for truth, the adventure of ideas, as learners and as teachers, freely and without fetters of dogma or prescription. This is what distinguishes a university from a trade school and a training camp, and this central characteristic of a university is important to grasp. Like many important ideas, it is often misunderstood. Nor, when recognized, is it always appreciated. Such misunderstanding is apparent, for example, when you hear a person say, "Well, why don't they just teach good, old, solid Americanism—or good, old-fashioned logic—or good, old, intelligible music —(or good, sound whatever it may be)?" What such a person wants is an institution restricted to traffic in those ideas with which he is comfortable. What he wants is indoctrination, not education. He fails to recognize that the university is a place where the search for truth and value must be unending.

So, also, when a person inveighs against a university because it does not offer training in surf-casting, or sales-promotion, or mink-ranching, he is revealing a distorted notion of it as a super-market rather than as a place of inquiry and investigation. Or, again, when someone sneers at the testimony of university professors as "too theoretical," he is really saying he distrusts theory, which is an aspect of hard thought and is precisely one of the prime things a university exists to nurture and pursue.

Why should a university *not* dispense dogma, *not* become a supermarket, *not* scorn theory? Because our civilization and the very existence of a free and open society require places where the adventurous, uninhibited search for improved knowledge—for rational understanding and rational principles—can be carried on.

Civilization has never been very secure on this globe; nor have the ideals of freedom and justice. Man has now walked on the moon, but despite the magnificent achievements of twentieth-century science and technology, he still walks with uncertainty and sometimes with fear on the earth.

THE MODERN UNIVERSITY is involved in no less than the survival of our civilization and the future of the human race. Indeed, it bears toward these grave issues a special responsibility: the development of the fresh talent and techniques and insights required better to comprehend and cope with them. No other institutions or agencies in our society are so particularly designed and dedicated to the large and essential task of searching for clarity and understanding, of trying to see the requirements of our civilization steadily and whole, of developing the root knowledge (and the men who can use it) on which wise action depends. It is the universities who are engaged in preserving and re-examining ideas and knowledge, always looking to the relation between the individual and the state. It is universities who insist on man's duty and right to think otherwise, and to say so—and who habitually seek to bring the light of reason to the understanding and conduct of human affairs. (I have used the pronoun "who" rather than "which" deliberately, to underscore the fact that persons, not places, perform these functions; that the university is a human institution.)

An imperfect organization at any time, old-fashioned in many ways, delicate in its internal relations, but with a remarkable capacity to endure, the university like the river boat in Conrad's *Heart of Darkness* is always pushing perilously into unknown regions, under attack by ignorant antagonists, but making the journey, and preparing for another.

As an institution in time and space the university cannot be immune to the effect of turbulence in the general society. It has, furthermore, the fundamental obligation to put the power of critical intelligence to work on society's problems— through both research and teaching.

Appropriate targets for the university's attention may lie close to home, and in too many cases perhaps, universities have overlooked the requirements of the immediate communities in which they stand in order to seek larger arenas and serve larger publics. Be that as it may, the university must expect today to be stirred from within by some who would lead it into direct forms of social action, and at the same time it must expect to be buffeted from without by individuals and institutions that somehow want instant solutions from it. With all this stirring and buffeting, it remains in everyone's best interest, I believe, for the university's response to be pointed in the main to that which is fundamental, of lasting relevance and far-reaching consequence, not focused in the main on immediate pressures and problems.

In *The Society of Man*, Louis Halle presents an image of the scholar's role which seems to me to express well this most critical function of the university in relation to society:

The scholar's business is direction. He is like the navigator of a ship, who does not himself take the wheel but makes the calculations on the basis of which the actions of the man at the wheel can be addressed, as opportunity serves, to a purpose beyond the immediate moment. If the sea is chaotic, the man at the wheel will have to be preoccupied with every looming wave that threatens the ship, and will have to act quickly either to evade or meet it, even though this means acting with apparent inconsistency, turning first in one direction, then in another. But these waves are not the navigator's business, and he will only confuse himself and the helmsman if he tries to make them his business. His business is to see beyond "the transient and the complicated," and to make known what he sees, so that the ship can in the long run realize a purpose beyond that of survival in the present, so that it can have direction.

I place special emphasis on reflection and the long view at this time because I believe there are questions before us so subtle that we cannot deal with them properly by *ad hoc* propositions, questions that press hard upon us all, new questions and age-old issues of right and wrong. The world has always been in need of thoughtful, reflective men of good will, concerned not simply with what will work but with what is true and what is right. It has never needed them more than now.

Nothing I have said is intended to downgrade professional or technical education. They belong in the university context when a commitment to searching thought and concern for fundamental principles lie behind them and feed actively into them. The surest guarantee that such a rationale is always at work is, I believe, nothing less than the placing of the arts and sciences, liberally conceived, at the center of the university's concern and enterprise. They tell us what the best of men have thought and felt and discovered in their furthest reaches of mind and imagination. They bring us into touch with those great currents of thought and understanding that, in the words of Woodrow Wilson, "beat down out of the old centuries into the new" and "constitute the pulse and life of the race."

Part of this pulse and life is the spirit of free-roving, critical inquiry coupled to an open view about the nature of truth. And it follows that a

root function of a university is that it be dedicated—stubbornly dedicated—to the pursuit of
improved knowledge, understanding, light, in all
of its teaching and all of its research.

Widely differing institutions profess to be universities. Too few live up to the name. Literally,
the word means "turned toward oneness, com-
bined into one," a union of persons with a common
interest. But today the forces which pull outward
often seem to be the stronger. Indeed, in many
ways, on many fronts, modern culture, like an
exploding universe, is moving out in diverse direc-
tions and threatens to become ever more atomistic.

Knowledge and the professions divide into
branches, specialties, sub-specialties, and sub-sub-
specialties. The once tidy house of intellect has
swollen until, as the late Professor Charles
Osgood put it, "it has burst into 10,000 fragments, and no turn of the academic kaleidoscope
could bring these fragments into a consistent or
lasting design." But as Professor Osgood further
observed, to surrender at that point would be "like
the man who gave up reading the encyclopedia
because he couldn't follow the story."

We cannot simply wring our hands in despair.
The problem of "the one" and "the many" is an
old problem, and there never has been a fully

satisfactory answer to it. Lacking a modern synthesis, we can perhaps nevertheless encourage more of our best minds to be concerned with the *need* for one. And we should press where we can, I believe, the search for coherence and relevance. Here I mean not simply concern for what is topical and current, but rather the cultivation of interrelationships—of interactions—both among the areas of learning and between them and life.

I**N OUR SEARCH** for balance between detachment and involvement we often hear the argument that the university should largely direct its teaching and research to what is *immediately* relevant. One recalls from pre-television days the "news-reel theaters," with their flickering glimpses of the latest events in the world. If one of those films were to be rerun for us today, we would be struck, I am sure, by the triviality and inconsequence of much that once seemed pressingly relevant. And just so, while some of our present national concerns are, indeed, awesome in their dimensions and future import, in a decade or two they may seem about as pertinent as the open-air trolley.

And so the university must take the long view, and men within it are properly concerned with the politics of Aristotle as well as of Mao, the history of science as well as the most rapidly advancing nuclear theory, the visions of Ovid and of Dante no less than those of Kafka and Ginsberg. All of these have their relevance.

This is not to suggest that the university should be an entirely serene retreat, sealed off from day-to-day life, its faculty members concerned only with the pure life of the mind (research and study unsullied by applicability), its students finding in the university both a sanctuary and a cocoon that bundles them up for gentle maturing and wards off to a future day all need to feel direct obligation to other men or to society.

The Roman poet Lucretius once expressed such a vision of the life of learning as something pure, elevated, and apart. In 1890 when Alexander Hall was added to the Princeton campus, someone appropriated two lines of that vision and caused them to be inscribed on the building's south face, where they stand boldly—and ignored!—today:

Nil dulcius est bene quam munita tenere Edita doctrina sapientum templa serena.

(Nothing is more pleasant than to occupy the calm high places secured by the teachings of the wise.)

Just six years later, when Princeton celebrated its 150th anniversary and took on the name of university, the controlling idea was markedly different. Then it was "Princeton in the Nation's Service," and the man who proclaimed it was Woodrow Wilson:

It is indispensable, it seems to me, if the university is to do its right service, that the air of affairs should be admitted to all its classrooms. I do not mean the air of party politics, but the air of the world's transactions . . . the sense of duty of man toward man, of the presence of men in every problem, of the significance of truth for guidance as well as for knowledge, of the potency of ideas, of the promise and the hope that shine in the face of all knowledge. There is laid upon us the compulsion of the national life. We dare not keep aloof and close ourselves while a nation comes into maturity. The days of glad expansion are gone, our life grown tense and difficult; our recourse for the future lies in careful thought, providence, and a wise economy, and the school must be of the nation.

IN SOME MEASURE at least, the modern university has helped to create the restless currents of this era. It has done so by its searching, inquisitive spirit and by the changes it has helped to effect—especially through science and technology—in the ways in which men think, work, communicate, and spend their leisure. In other ways too, what happens in universities these days has great consequence outside their classrooms and laboratories. Industry, government, and the professions all depend heavily upon the knowledge, insight, skills, and talents which are cultivated and made available in universities. Likewise, personal achievement for the individual and successful attack upon our country's gravest domestic problems—poverty, racism, and urban blight—all depend increasingly on them.

In its parts and as a whole, then, the university must be sensitive to the needs of the larger communities to which it belongs. It must be judiciously responsive to those needs which it can effectively help to meet *as a university*. But let us never forget that its cardinal function is to be a place where searching inquiry and sober reflection are the order of the day. All other activities of a university properly grow out of these. And for that to be true, a considerable degree of detachment (which is a very different thing from indifference) must be possible both for faculty and students.

The university must stand, in part, apart. It must do this because it is society's main testing ground for ideas, both in its teaching and in its scholarship, and is the surest agency men have yet found for this precious freedom-making activity. When the university tries to become a lobby or a pressure-group forcing the processes of government, or when it saddles itself with a multitude of tasks of merely current relevance, it both jeopardizes its claim and reduces its competence to be itself: a center for rational analysis, criticism, and pathfinding.

Although the university performs a unique and essential role for society, it is nevertheless often beset by the overly timid and backward-looking who—made uneasy by the university's innovative and critical functions and troubled by what they regard as a widespread "dissolution of authority" —wish to put strict curbs on it. They tend to accept vocational training and "mental discipline," but in the main they seek to cut the university off from everything but the function of preserving and purveying received knowledge.

There are others who in their restiveness about

the persistent ills of our society and anger at its continuing injustices wish to "politicize" the university and make it a direct instrument of social struggle. Believing that the ends justify the means, they have little hesitation about inviting political and social turmoil to the campus.

In my view, the partisans in each of these two camps are about equally misguided and dangerous. The university cannot—as has been observed —survive as an arena where gladiatorial groups fight to the death, where violent pressures toward reform and unyielding resistance to reform produce either upheaval or paralysis, or both. And it must be recognized that a university is very easy to disrupt. It is held together neither by steel cables nor enforceable laws. All that holds it together are good will, tolerance, and a common respect both for reason and for reasonableness.

IF I HAVE SEEMED to be viewing the detachment–involvement tension as one chiefly troubling university presidents or faculties, let me say that I am only too aware that every sensitive student also feels its pull, feels it far more keenly than did his counterpart of twenty, or ten, or even five years ago. He must ask himself whether his university experience should be a time spent in relative isolation from the world or a time of close involvement in movements and causes, not excluding the running of the university itself. A number of young—and not so young—people now assert that the universities simply do not represent actuality; that students can get in touch with the actual only by *doing something*, as if learning were not an act; and that existing universities are obsolete and irrelevant.

All of this is to fail to see them for what they essentially are: not production lines to be retooled for today's fashion, not governments to be voted in or out, but delicate yet lasting associations whose prime commitment is to the virtue of thought in mankind's long, tortured endeavor to build a fairer and more peaceable world. The university is critical of old ideas, skeptical of present wisdom, and passionate for new knowledge. The university does not say: "Believe this—here is the word!" It says: "Look, ask, and search! Here is accumulated knowledge, and here are ways in which men are endeavoring to correct it, improve it, and make it more useful. The findings of any time are not infallible, but they are likely to be the best answers available, and sometimes they emerge with sharp clarity to cast a whole new light on some aspect of knowledge or human affairs."

It is easy to be scornful of institutions, but if we are to live effectively in today's world we must live and work within them; and it is to the institutions called universities that we must look for the education of the individuals—scientists, artists, lawyers, doctors, ministers, teachers, and others— on whom depend the advancement and improvement of civilized life.

Sir Arthur Lewis, of the Princeton faculty, spoke to this whole matter with telling insight and eloquence when he was installed as Chancellor of the University of Guyana:

The human race has pulled itself up . . . by handing down from generation to generation knowledge of two sets of principles, those relating to controlling nature, which we call science, and principles relating to human behavior, which we call ethics. Human life as we know it today is based on accumulated science, and accumulated ethical principles enshrined in laws and in the conventions of decent behavior.

The supremely important task of receiving this knowledge, adding to it, and handing it down to the next generation has always devolved on a very small body of people, who specialize in using their brains. They were known as clerks . . . the ethical and cultural values which we clerks preserve are like a thin veneer, easily rubbed off by mass hatreds and ignorance. In 1933 Germany, the most scientific nation in Europe, went barbarous overnight. . . . Genocide has become the favorite crime of our century; Turks and Armenians, Germans and Jews, Hindus and Muslims, Jews and Arabs, Hausas and Ibos—a melancholy list, which alas is probably not yet ended. The clerks have always had a hard time keeping civilization going, and it doesn't become any easier.

Here we come to the fundamental purpose of education: to produce young men and women who will join the band of clerks stretching backward through history and forward to generations yet unborn. Who will receive our truths, embellish them, defend them against numerous and powerful enemies, and pass them on to the next generation? If our graduates do not help to keep civilization together, to reduce the sum of human misery, and to advance the cause of human brotherhood, then our university will have labored in vain.

SOME ARGUE that the nation's problems are so pressing that a young person's obligation to engage himself in their solution *now* overrides his obligation to his university studies, or any good these studies can help him do later on. The premise that urgent and massive problems confront us cannot be denied; the signals are clear. But from this premise it does not necessarily follow that students should divert a major part of their limited time and energy from study to action at this stage of their lives. The future calls not for eager improvisers but for minds trained in fundamental studies, able to cut deeply, and take the long view.

Final responsibility is a lonely business. When one faces it, no handbooks or even computers can suffice. All one can draw on is his experience, his education, his ability to think, his sensitivity to others' problems, and his faith in man's ability to order his life better. Here is where his university experience, if he has let himself really experience it, can steady him, can let him know that he is not alone on his journey, that what happened yesterday or ten thousand yesterdays ago has something to do with what happens tomorrow. I am not urging students to spend their college years staring into a rear-view mirror or to divest themselves of social concern. On the contrary, they should be looking around and ahead as well as back, and pondering hard the deep, vexing, moral, social, and spiritual issues of our times.

There can be fruitful interplay throughout one's life between the incentives to action and to reflection. The student is in a unique position to reflect so that he may in the future act with more wisdom and more telling effect. My plea, then, is that he not look on his studies as the "execution of intellectual minuets," but as the means of developing his best resources, and his convictions, for tough jobs ahead. The role of the student, taken seriously, is one of the most important in the modern world.

A student may say, "Yes, yes, I buy all that. I want to be detached enough to concentrate on my studies. But how can any sane person concentrate on anything but immediate dangers in a period as dangerous as this?"

Well—"into the dangerous world, I leapt," wrote Blake, and he was right: The world has never been a safe, sane, or tidy place. The prospect of thermonuclear holocaust is indeed ghastly; but it is only the hideous and gigantic unfolding, to whole populations, of the frightful, dehumanizing nature and consequences of war down through the ages. To the shame of mankind, and despite the message of Christ, wars and threats of wars have occupied much of human history. Famine, pestilence, and suffering have been the lot of millions upon millions of human beings over the ages, and are so today. To establish, safeguard, and extend the government of free men by themselves, with due respect for the dignity of the individual —these have always been perilous and arduous undertakings. We are not the first men to be faced by strong antagonistic forces operating both in covert and in overt ways, nor the first to be called upon to show clarity of mind and steadiness of purpose under conditions of extreme strain.

It is in some such perspective as this, I suggest, that students ought to view the opportunity they have to be students: to inhabit a place where the spirit of dispassionate inquiry and the search for the long view prevail; amid the turmoil and tenseness of the immediate present, to extend their ground and competence for a more cool-headed and more far-reaching appraisal of themselves and of this mixed-up world. This chance is given them at a time in their lives when their eyes are clearer, their hands cleaner, their ability to grow in reasoned understanding greater than probably ever again.

Suppose we were to produce a generation of

university graduates who were no more than trained specialists, unconcerned with the fundamental principles on which their specialties rest and on which their very civilization rests; unaccustomed to thinking about such matters; to whom almost all of history, philosophy, and literature—the record of man's acts and insights—would seem irrelevant. Try to imagine the fate of our democratic nation, conceived in liberty yet confronted with an ideology determined to destroy that liberty, needing men and women able to exercise sophisticated judgment—at the polls, in management, in legislatures—yet finding that our new generation of higher and lower level technicians did not know how to exercise sophisticated judgment, how to evaluate, how to take the long view; and, worse, did not know that they did not know!

In combat situations there are commonly certain ground troops designated as "forward observers." Theirs is a dangerous and often lonely assignment, for it is their job to be out ahead, seeing far and clearly, spotting targets, passing back needed information; and often they are called upon to make difficult decisions. I like to think of a truly educated man as a forward observer, trained in his special assignment, but with his view focused ahead, and the welfare of many others depending upon his vision, his steadiness, and his judgment.

D O I SEEM to be favoring detachment over involvement as a student attitude? Then let me put in a word for something that impels our best students toward involvement: something I can only call the spirit of discontent. Not the discontent that inspires rebellion just for rebellion's sake, that sends young people out on petulant window-breaking sprees, but rather discontent informed by intelligence and conscience, discontent that comes of recognizing and rejecting what is unworthy of us as human beings.

This true and more mature discontent, this thoughtful indignation, is the spirit that pierces self-deception, that is not satisfied with things as they are, that seeks always to render them better —or, at least, better understood. It accepts the necessity of sacrifice and hard work this side of Eden, and it is closely related to the spirit of freedom under whose institutions the readiness to question, to explore change, and to seek a better way can flourish. As such, the true spirit of discontent is one of the strongest and most creative forces working for civilization, for human dignity.

Aristophanes, Juvenal, and the later great satirists of eighteenth-century England and France were moved by this kind of discontent to dissect not in order to destroy, but because they had a larger and better vision of the way men might be. To be sure, the spirit of discontent with its manifestations in free debate and vigorous criticism may sometimes be hard to take. I can testify that in some student editorials of recent years it has quite spoiled my morning coffee. But in the long run we cannot survive without it, this capability of the human mind to see clearly, to judge objectively, and to demand a possible better instead of settling for what is. Without this motive force primitive man would never have substituted the wheel for the sled, Greeks would not have evolved democratic processes of government, Romans of the empire would not have troubled to develop an impartial system of law, Englishmen would not have struggled to achieve freedom of speech and limitations on the powers of government, art would have languished and science would have been unknown. And may I say that this creative discontent tends to exist more dynamically in the young than in their elders—perhaps because a good deal of sheer energy is required to fuel it!

We are being prodded today by young people deeply concerned about basic things, and in them we find the searching discontent which demands of us better, more thoughtful, more vital responses. Daily and in thousands of ways—in the home, on the job, in work for their communities and for the nation, both here and abroad—these young men and women give renewed expression to the moral and spiritual strength of our country, the progressive nature of our heritage.

My hope is that more of us of all ages will begin to take these concerns seriously. It seems to me urgent that we should. For if we are to advance our potentially dynamic ideals of freedom for the individual, the worth of the person, and equal justice under the law, then we shall have to make contest for them in an intelligent and determined way through almost every act and fact of our lives, both here in this country and around the globe.

3

CONSERVATION &
INNOVATION

INSOFAR AS THE university is called upon to be both detached and involved, one might say that it must look, at the same time, both inward and outward. Let me speak now of a tension that requires the university to look simultaneously both backward and forward: to be always both a conservative and an innovative force in the world.

The word "conservative" has been preempted of late by some who do injustice to its proper sense. I claim it for that activity of the university which upholds what is found to be true, to be consistent, to be of worth to man in his relations to his fellows and to his physical environment. Rightly understood and exercised, this process of conservation in the university is not a miser-like hovering over dead learning, not like the school-men Bacon described as "fierce with dark keeping." It is an engagement in those great currents of thought and knowledge that flow down to us out of the past, constantly renewing, transforming, evolving, enduring, as central and precious components of civilized life. And, above all, the self-renewing life of the untrammeled mind—the right of man to know and seek knowledge freely —is what the university seeks to conserve.

Today, as in every age of restlessness and uncertainty, these deep, vital currents of the mind and spirit desperately need safe-guarding. Men grasp for the quick, packaged solution. Practicality readily becomes mere expediency. Assertions of materialism and determinism press hard upon us. At the same time that we would protect the right of defenders of such positions to be heard, we know that the direction of their reductive and insulting views of the nature of man is toward the paralysis and degradation of the spirit, and prepares the undisciplined mind for stark conformity. Best and most fully, if not alone, among our secular institutions, the universities can give us nobler and better founded estimates of man's potential and set us to work toward goals beyond the daily routine, the muddle, the temporary stalemate.

Our artists, our free press, our political debates also have critical roles to play in the never-ending struggle to preserve the free flow of ideas and in the task of keeping alive the best of what men have thought and felt and discovered in their furthest reaches of mind and imagination; but in all this the role of universities today is pivotal.

Years ago, some universities were guardians in another, more physical sense. The medieval institutions of Paris and Oxford were formed by scholars who came together for association, but also for protection. The ancient castle and remains of the city wall at Oxford are reminders that gown and town were not immune to attack by armed force as well as by subtler agents. Witness the removal by Parliament of some four hundred fellows and scholars from the Oxford colleges during the purges of the mid-seventeenth century. In 1653, the Barebones Parliament actually threatened to confiscate the colleges and universities. In reply a spokesman for the universities, Seth Ward, upheld vigorously their need "to follow the Banner of truth by whomsoever it shall be lifted up."

"The Banner of truth" is, however, unlike most banners. In its train march not only guardians of the heritage of the past, not only defenders against all attacks on the life of the mind, but also champions of new causes and advancers of knowledge still unknown. Often the same people play all these parts at once. And here we come back to one of the paradoxes which lies at the heart of the university's unique existence—the fact that it is an innovating and revolutionary force at the same time that it is a conserver and guardian. The resultant, inherent, and continuing tension is not conducive to serenity. If the students are well taught, they will learn to do their own thinking and not simply accept what is handed to them. Even as they learn about the past, they should be using the knowledge to extend and strengthen their powers of analysis and judgment for matters yet to come. As someone once said, in universities men should be constantly in the process of making up their minds and then unmaking them.

There will always be many outside the institution who fail to see that the search for new truths and the encouragement of independent thought in students are the proper business of the university. And students within the university may themselves often be uncomfortable in the presence of so much uncertainty and dissent, especially in those moments when what they most want is "the cold dope" and a passbook to good grades. But comfort and docility are not adequate criteria either for oneself or for the university. When that mood is on him, let the student bear in mind these words of the late Judge Learned Hand:

> As soon as we cease to pry about at random, we shall come to rely upon accredited bodies of authoritative dogma; and as soon as we come to rely upon accredited bodies of authoritative dogma, not only are the days of our liberty over, but we have lost the password that has hitherto opened the gates of success as well.

Indeed, an irreplaceable service of the university in a free society is to nurture individuals and ideas that can stand against the dreariness of conformity and the darkness of absolutism, and still live and work in concert with one another.

In this role the university may find itself in trouble. From the time of Socrates, the innovating thinker and the independent mind have encountered resistance—whether urging reform of the state, the sun as center of our solar system, anesthesia in childbirth, or a radically different esthetic principle. I reiterate these facts to emphasize that, like a sometimes excentric, sometimes noisome family, a university needs to be understood, and there is constant need for support, interpretation, and defense by those who bear allegiance to her.

It is in some ways humbling, in other ways encouraging and comforting, to look back. It greatly improves one's perspective and judgment of current problems to read, for example, this lamentation—"Our youths now love luxury. They have bad manners, contempt for authority, disrespect for older people. They no longer rise when their elders enter the room. They contradict their parents, . . . and tyrannize their teachers"—and to realize that it was not made yesterday by a university president, but reportedly by Socrates in the fifth century B.C., the so-called Golden Age of Greek culture.

We are told continually, and we know, that things are changing very rapidly today, and there is a temptation to believe that the past has little relevance. But the university is founded on the belief that the best way for anyone to effect change of any lasting kind is to begin by truly educating himself, becoming well-acquainted with history's heights and depths, and with the full dimensions of what he is trying to do. This brings us to fundamentals and the long view. Man has a noble potential, but he also possesses a vast capacity for error. He has played the brute as often as the saint, and an awareness of these radical ambiguities in him is essential to anyone who would make sensible innovations. Which is to say that before he enters the lists, one should be prepared to forswear the easy rhetoric of self-righteous arrogance.

A friend of mine was fond of saying, "If you want to persuade someone to your view, you can't afford to be more than 85 per cent right." It must be the awareness of human fallibility we all carry within us that makes the man without error so obnoxious to most of us. Surely we have all experienced the irritation evoked by the person who acts as though he had his own pipeline to the Almighty, the man so thoroughly persuaded of his own rectitude that he will not even discuss how he achieved it. Claims put forth from such a posture usually founder in a chasm of hostility created by the posture itself.

Militant self-righteousness is, of course, not new in the human record. Philosophical and theological history acquaint us with the heresy of antinomianism and the various guises in which it has appeared from the early Christian era to modern times. The antinomian aberration takes the form of a passionate conviction that your relation to the deity is so intense and perfect as to have put you in a state of grace which sets you above both the Mosaic code and the civil law. Centuries elapsed between the first strong appearance of antinomianism and the second, but the cycles seem to have shortened after the Renaissance. Now it has been 150 years since theological antinomianism last was seriously espoused. In secular forms, though, there seems to be a lot of it loose today.

W E ARE ALL in part products of past history, even when we are not aware of it. Most of the dominant trends of our times—social, economic, political, cultural— began long ago and will not finally work themselves out until long after we are gone.

When he was Dean of Princeton's Graduate School, Professor Colin S. Pittendrigh often took his biologist's lens to the problems he faced in the area of educational policy and administration. I recall an analogy he once drew between the evolution of organisms and of organizations.

All living organisms have built-in mechanisms which help them to adapt to new conditions, he said; and a key factor in the process of evolution is the rate at which an organism manages to adapt. To survive, it must be able to react quickly enough to new circumstances. The same is true of human organizations, including colleges and universities. There come times when they must be ready to respond to new conditions, to modify or even abandon old habits and old notions. We must be prepared to hear, and not fear, the calls to newer, more challenging uplands. To dig our heels in and resist institutional evolution is to invite stagnation and extinction.

But there is another side to the matter. Just as a biological organism can perish from reacting too little or too late, it can also do itself in by reacting too fast and too much. The organisms that survive have a kind of built-in conservatism that protects them from such moves. Professor Pittendrigh reminds us that extinction has, in fact, befallen the too-ready innovator more often than the too-stubborn conserver.

The parallel for the world of learning is clear, and helps to explain why colleges and universities are sometimes stubbornly change-resistant. It has been said that the only thing harder to move than a curriculum is a graveyard, and I myself confess to having felt at times a similar impotence in my dealings with the Princeton faculty. But educators are properly wary of changing capriciously, of reacting just for the sake of doing so, and of ignoring roots which are vital to continued sustenance. Misguided response of such a sort can lead to forgotten backwashes where the chief purpose a thing serves is ultimately to offer up its fossil remains for study. And that's hardly an end any of us would deliberately seek.

A mark of the educated man is his ability to hold two opposing ideas in mind simultaneously and not be paralyzed by them. His characteristic point of view on a great many things is "both . . . and," not simply "either . . . or." And when this dual vision is informed, focused, and functioning well, like the stereoscope applied to aerial photographs, it causes ideas and events to emerge in their full dimensions and with a clarity not otherwise found.

Consider, for example, what it is that we *most* want a student to learn. On the one hand, we want him to learn to think for himself, to be passionate for new knowledge, to be eager to test old knowledge and, when he can, to improve on it. As John Milton observed: "The light which we have gained was given us not to be ever staring on, but by it to discover onward things more remote from our knowledge." So a spirit of ceaseless quest, of restless inquiry and of innovation is an essential element in liberal education. And if this leads a student sometimes to think radically, to be a bit revolutionary, we really should not be surprised.

All the while, however, liberal education also seeks to foster an awareness and appreciation of the things of enduring worth. The study of the present, not girded under with knowledge of the past, is both shallow and fragile. Learning is dead when it is not illumined by a sense of relevance to the things of ultimate human concern.

But docility and self-satisfaction have little place in a liberal college or university. There should be controversy and arguing and a great deal of churning of matters of mind and spirit. Out of such a millrace of jostling and tumbling ideas comes the kind of tough, honed intellect that recognizes and wishes to do battle with the imperfections of the world, but harbors no illusions that there are easy remedies for them.

Today among our young people there is widespread dissatisfaction with the state of the world and of our country. In my view, much of this is immensely healthy and is consonant with the high idealism of our origins as a free people.

There are, to be sure, ugly currents in the waves of student unrest sweeping our campuses. Some of it is simply and deliberately pernicious.

Even when unrest is not malicious, to make oneself the champion of righteous causes can be dangerously heady business, and what too often suffers is respect for the views and rights of others. (But this is no new phenomenon: "Truth," William Penn noted, "often suffers more by the heat of its defenders, than from the arguments of its opposers.") In the name of sincerity and conviction, absolutists both inside and outside our campuses press extreme demands and seek to bring the house down. Indeed, sometimes those of the radical right and those of the radical left seem to have stretched around full circle to occupy the same portion of the field, where all that can be heard is one angry snarl.

But we should not let the venom and anarchism of a small segment of the student activists blind us to the positive aspects of the situation: the heartening idealism, the genuine concern for the quality of our national life, the antipathy to man's exploitation of man that is so evident among today's students. Gone, in large measure, is the flatulent complacency that we bemoaned in students only a few years back. Not in my experience, or in my reading, has there been a college generation more acutely aware of the persistent ills of our society and more eager to do something about them.

If educating liberally includes stirring things up a bit and setting individuals thinking, then it probably follows that the more genuine education an individual possesses, the harder it is to keep him in his place. In this respect, we educators surely are part of the cause for some of the stir and activity on today's campuses.

Our task now, it seems to me, is not to worry about how to "keep students in their place" and "stamp out student activism." It is rather to try to face squarely the legitimate questions of younger people impatient with the imperfections they see all around them. It is to help them channel constructively their desire to do something about the state of the world. I would add that, in the spirit of liberal learning, this involves helping them to acquire a humble respect both for their own limitations and for the rights and capacities of others— including even those over thirty. Perfection may be the lot of angels; it is not that of men. Conversely, good will, high purpose, and determination to reduce man's inhumanity to man are not the sole possessions of any age-group, race, or faction.

Educating liberally for today and tomorrow

means keeping an even tension—in teaching no less than in learning—between the long view and fundamental learning at one end of the bow, and at the other, the closely felt requirements of the ever more complicated, ever more demanding world we live in.

No other institution in our society is so clearly dedicated to this purpose as is the university. To be sure, public libraries, independent research institutes, laboratories, museums, and various government panels and bureaus all help to advance and to transmit knowledge. But none of these combines in quite the same way as do the universities the functions of vigorously and simultaneously advancing new knowledge, opening fresh insights into old knowledge, and helping to preserve the best that men have managed to think and do, down the long reaches of human effort. None is so concerned to lead students to discovering what it means to possess, in Professor Hubert Alyea's words, "a prepared mind." None is so dedicated to guarding that precious thing in our society, the spirit of free inquiry.

THE MINDS needed to lead us through the present and future turmoil will not be produced by a curriculum, or a package of courses, a preordained selection of subjects, or any magic total of credit hours. The liberal education required is far more helpfully seen as a process and an aspiration, and here I borrow back from a statement of Dr. Conant's, which he borrowed from a colleague of mine, who says that he got some of it from me. (You can call this a meeting of minds, or academic license.)

Embedded in the concept of a liberal education, as it has been held in varying ways over the centuries, there is something we may recognize and value. But it does not inhere in a program or pattern. We are close to the mark if we conceive of it as a process and as aspiration. A liberal education, one might say, is a process begun in childhood, carried on through a varying number of years of schooling, and best tested by the momentum it sustains in adult life. It is characterized by what it aspires to, rather than by what it embraces; it aims to enlarge the understanding, to develop respect for data, and to strengthen the ability to think and act rationally. . . . It seeks to produce an informed, inquiring, and judicious habit of mind rather than particular abilities.

In reaching toward these aims, some universities have been successful and continue to be successful in a remarkable degree. Never before, in my years on the Princeton campus, have I found students generally to be so actively concerned with learning. And there is evidence of the same eagerness on other campuses. Indeed, a part of the current student discontent with established curricula—however flexible a given curriculum may be—is a desire for self-education, for relevance to one's own interests, for self-discovery, which is both natural and very healthy.

Moreover, the improvement in so many of our schools in the teaching of languages, mathematics, science, history, and literature are resulting in a breed of college students prepared to deal with these subjects well above the levels of my generation at the same age. Meantime, the rapid increase of knowledge daily makes obsolete parts of the older learning, older data, and older methodologies.

Putting this all together—the eagerness of students for self-education, their heightened preparation and wider horizons, and the steady advance of knowledge—our colleges and universities face a challenge and an opportunity unequalled in the history of education. Our best guideline in trying to meet this challenge and this opportunity is, I believe, to emphasize encouragement of the student to develop a *continuing* rational curiosity— that is, to be a learner all his life.

A liberal education should make the student want to act and to play a part in the shaping of our society and the raising of its tone and style. At times, a heightened awareness of the gaps between our society's ideals and its accomplishments will make students angry; that can be all to the good. A righteous anger may lead to fanaticism, but with liberality it can spur the determination to enlist constructively in the ranks of those who, as the Urban Coalition asks, "give a damn." But at the same time the educated man must always be aware that there are no easy panaceas for the tough problems and conditions of life. The trained intelligence is immensely useful and the need for it is greater every day, but even it is no magic key. History is replete with examples of this hard reality.

Education, as it enlarges awareness of life's

complexities and lays on the young person what Woodrow Wilson called "the burden of other people's business," very often will make the road ahead harder. Denied to the liberally educated man will be the pat solutions and the simplistic sloganeering that serve so many and are so very misleading. Instead he will find that genuine progress is usually a tortuously slow business, and that often the compromise accepting of "half-a-loaf" is the wisest course. This is by no means always pleasant medicine. Other generations have not always liked it either when, in Samuel Johnson's phrase, they were "towering in the confidence of twenty-one."

Yet the facts are inescapable. Part of the dream must remain tentative. An important part of the learning process is discovering the wide disparity between professed ideals and actual performance, and coming to recognize that a gap between aspiration and accomplishment is one of the tragic conditions of human life. This the wisest men have known and have not despaired. It reduces not a bit the importance of trying to narrow the gap and build a more sane, just, peaceful world.

I T IS THE UNIVERSITY's responsibility to bring about sound innovation in every field, and this includes its own; that is, the field of higher education.

Of the aims of a liberal education, probably the most critical, as I have said, is that of providing the impetus or momentum that makes an individual want to go on inquiring and learning long after his formal education ends. Perhaps it would be more accurate to say that this is the aspect of a liberal education with which we have succeeded least well, but which today is of the most heightened importance because of the rate at which advancing knowledge makes inadequate and obsolete old theories, methodologies, and assemblages of data.

The difficulties posed by this acceleration are perhaps more acutely felt from the standpoint of curricular planning in the sciences than in the humanities, where the great body of works of literature and art and the material of philosophy appropriate for undergraduate study are not so vast that intelligent selection is impossible—though here certainly our former preoccupation with the history and thought of the western world is no longer adequate. But the problem of choosing and organizing the subjects to be covered and the materials to be taught is far more complex and difficult in the natural sciences, as it is also in the newer, quantitative aspects of the social sciences. In these fields education feels itself plagued, as it were, by the rapidity of the turnover in methodology, in the data which are judged to be relevant, in the theories that are agreed on as valid.

My point is that the momentum sustained in later life is at once a key attribute of liberal education and a touchstone insufficiently used and attended to within the academic fraternity. I suggest that it might be worth our time and energy to try to identify, however broadly and imprecisely, the kinds of studies *and the ways of inducting students into those studies* that seem to "take," get under the skin, give the student the habits of inquiry and reading and reflection that will stay with him. I would not resuscitate progressive education's error of subordinating everything to the student and his unfledged interests. We face here one of the oldest enigmas in education, but still an essential question: What can we do to influence a man to *want* to learn and *to go on learning*? Perhaps the investigation I suggest can yield no measurable results, but I can think of some large sums of money and a great deal of effort that have been spent on far less important educational matters.

I suggest that we be less ambitious for "breadth," placing less confidence in synoptic courses which attempt to pre-digest great areas of knowledge, and that we settle for smaller domains which invite curiosity and make vivid the need for discipline and method, even while they illustrate general issues and principles.

Recognizing the diversity of students, the significant improvement of academic programs in many high schools, the pressure of time on the undergraduate years, I would propose further that for some of our undergraduates we might well take a leaf from the book of the doctoral program. I mean install general examinations in one or more major divisions of knowledge as alternatives to general education or distribution requirements. If universities and colleges would take a fraction of the time and money they now spend on survey courses and spend it on reading lists and examinations for which students could largely prepare themselves, they might accomplish more for many students than they now do.

As to the "depth" element in undergraduate education, I would insist upon its greater importance; for, as A. N. Whitehead once observed, "In edu-

cation as elsewhere a broad primrose path leads
to a nasty place." But there can be no doubt that
at most institutions many if not all so-called "major" programs need a hard look, to see whether
they do in fact offer the sequential development of
the field that they claim, whether they are truly
capable of being examined comprehensively, and
whether they really constitute opportunities "to
learn one thing well." Here, I realize, we may tread
on some highly sensitive departmental toes. But
a rigorous examination of some of these sacrosanct
and often very costly "major" programs is, I suspect, long overdue.

My suggestion is simply this: that we who believe in the idea of a liberal education should not
go on the defensive but make every effort to develop and show its worth. This carries an important corollary—namely that, insofar as we can, we
see that our money goes where our mouths are.
When we do so, we have all the force of reason
and common sense behind us. The faster the advance and splintering of knowledge; the greater
the complexities of our lives, of our society, and of
the world in which we live; the further and more
rapidly technology and science thrust forward, the
more critical is the need for men and women who
carry in themselves respect for reason and disci-

plined thought, who have caught the habit of inquiry and reflection, who recognize the difference between knowledge and wisdom, and who know, too, how often pretensions to the latter are specious when not based upon the former.

L ET ME END this chapter on Conservation & Innovation by pointing out that man's opportunity to innovate under nearly ideal conditions is one of the things the university must conserve. The members of a university must be constantly sensitive to the need to protect the individual: his freedom; his person; his creative potential; his right to think and act responsibly, according to the dictates of his own conscience and reason, and—so long as he does no injury to others—to have his privacy of belief and person inviolate. And there must be an awareness that those who think or write or speak outside the dominant patterns of an era may yet be right.

All around us there are strong pressures in favor of low-level sorts of conformity, toward acceptance of the easy and the commonplace; pressures against unorthodoxy, individuality, and self-won responsibility. But the university is one place where happily it is (or should be) possible for men and women to think and act as their own best conscience and judgment dictate. Here it is that the willingness to think otherwise, to dream, to question, and to dare should flourish and have every appropriate outlet. If an utter stranger to our civilization should ask: "Where in your society can a person disagree with impunity from accepted practices, dogmas, and doctrines?" the answer should be, "In the universities."

Inevitably some of the varied forces that work against both personal independence and responsibility lurk and intrude among us in universities today. We are by no means totally advanced beyond the rule of the jungle or that of the herd— and we probably never shall be. Sometimes these forces make themselves felt subtly; at others, blindly and crudely. In whatever appearance, they require of us that constant, thoughtful sensitivity and vigilance which form the conditions upon which the enjoyment of liberty and dignity is accorded to man. Indeed, the only appropriate ethic in this sort of community is one that rests upon respect for the diversity and worth of individuals. When any one of us breaches these principles, or is casual about them, then we suffer collectively;

and we cease to uphold as well as we must that larger free society which we would serve.

Yet liberty itself needs to know limits, or it becomes anarchy and defeats itself. [Tension within tension: There is inevitably a strong cross-pull between the impulse to free expression and the need to respect institutions—and regulations—which must exist in order to safeguard freedom's being and right to expression.] Dissent which strikes out against all comers and on any occasion is blind, and of necessity sooner or later it draws strong counteraction against itself. It offers no adequate basis for a communality in which the freedom of the individual can flourish together with its proper companion, care for the rights and worth of others.

Even as these prime values require for their realization in society the services and safeguarding of institutions that possess appropriate limiting and punitive powers, so, too—and even more basically—they require within the members of the society a sense of respect for, and responsibility towards, their fellow men—felt in the heart, the gut, and the mind. Mahatma Gandhi once said, "Turn the searchlight inward. When my fellow man does wrong, it is in part my fault for not having improved him."

4

TEACHING & RESEARCH

THE DEMAND for new knowledge is inexhaustible, and this takes us into still another tension, the dual demand on our universities for teaching and research; and here Heraclitus' metaphor of the lyre is especially appropriate. Brought into effective interaction, teaching and scholarship produce a harmony that cannot be achieved by either separately. Pursued together, they generate an atmosphere of learning that invigorates and gives added point to both. This ideal harmony is not easily achieved, however, and is not likely to be achieved at all unless all of us in universities recognize the counter-pulls and see that they are balanced.

Most of what I have to say here of this tension will be in support of teaching, since in spite of growing pressure from students the pull of research today still seems to be the stronger. But let me begin with some observations about research.

Few who are successful in any field wish to spend every hour of the day dealing with the elementary things of their profession or business. They are glad to lead along younger men, to help them master the routines and proven techniques which have to be known, but there are also the subtleties of more advanced work which interest them, and more complicated challenges to meet. So it is with university teaching. Had he spent all his time on that log, Mark Hopkins would never have been the great teacher he was. Great teachers have left their enduring impact because their minds were on-going, searching minds, always alive to the deep unresolved mysteries of experience, always seeking a deeper insight into their quarter of the infinite domain of truth.

This was all said best perhaps by an Indian teacher and poet, Rabindranath Tagore, in a quotation which is one of my favorites:

> . . . a teacher can never truly teach unless he is still learning himself. A lamp can never light another lamp unless it continues to burn its own

flame. The teacher who has come to the end of his subject, who has no living traffic with his knowledge but merely repeats his lesson to his students can only load their minds; he cannot quicken them. Truth not only must inform but must inspire. If the inspiration dies out, and the information only accumulates, then truth loses its infinity.

A one-time Princeton president, Francis L. Patton, put it this way:

> The professor who has ceased to learn is unfit to teach . . . the man who sees nothing before him to kindle his own enthusiasm will chill the little enthusiasm a student may carry. . . .

Education works best when it draws on men who are content neither with the role of drill master nor of confectioner, but are themselves explorers. The spirit of inquiry in them, their love and hunger for truth, are a contagion which carries in everything they do.

We know that the best teachers are those who are also active in the search for new knowledge and deepened insights. But can we say more precisely what "good teaching" actually is?

In the educational journals its definition seems always to elude those who would capture it and pin it to the dissecting table—and it may well elude me. This is not surprising, for there are many kinds of good teaching, in many kinds of teaching situations, at many different levels. Attempts to reduce it to a formula are doomed to failure. There will always be teachers who will break all our rules and yet be profoundly successful. In other words, it is the good teacher, not teaching in the abstract, that counts.

This is not to say that the art of teaching cannot be studied or its skills conveyed, but rather that good teaching can never be successfully dealt with in a mechanical way. "Objective criteria" and "scientific evaluations" are attractive slogans to some in the world of education who are uneasy with anything that is not measurable. But such approaches to so complex and personal a thing as good teaching will always fall short. What is important is the *recognition* of it.

And here, I think, we should reject emphatically the proposition that "hearsay" is somehow not admissible or legitimate in judging teaching. How, really, do we ever recognize a great teacher? By the spoken testimony of hundreds of students and colleagues. It may have been diligently sought, carefully sifted and examined, and yet it remains hearsay. Apart from their scholarly writing, much of what we know of the teaching geniuses of all periods—Joseph Henry lecturing on electrical magnetism at Princeton, Mark Hopkins on the legendary log, Louis Agassiz in his zoological laboratory at Harvard, or Socrates in the market place—is based largely on hearsay.

Is this not perhaps another way of saying that the successful teacher is known by the mark he leaves on his students? If so, it is *not* the mark of indoctrination. (Someone has described the indoctrinal sort of teaching as pouring from a big pitcher into many little pitchers, then via the final examination back into the big pitcher.) No, the kind of teaching that is significant at the college or university level is not indoctrination.

When Louis Agassiz was asked his greatest achievement, he replied that he had taught men to observe. Socrates taught men to question. Each great teacher has his own way. Yet I suspect that more often than not two particular attributes will be found in the successful teacher. One is an ability to awaken and stimulate delight in the use of the mind. The second is attention to the *effort* to do so, together with a belief in its value to the student in his own right. Certainly those teachers I myself have admired most seem to have engendered in their students a pleasure, a joy, an increased awareness, in intellectual activity. Perhaps their students were not always the keenest of observers or the most skillful interlocutors, but they had discovered the pleasure of following ideas, the satisfaction in discovering where they lead, the lift in the journey that raises one above the misty flats of his own experience.

This does not always come easily either to student or to teacher. Undertaking to deal seriously with ideas is often a difficult job for the young (even under the best tutelage); and it is always a demanding and often lonely necessity for the teacher (even with the best of students). But vital connections do occur. Somehow the maturity of the teacher gets translated to the students so that they go beyond their years; it is conveyed to them in everything the good teacher writes and says.

There is another role that the good teacher plays. He is interpreter in the house of learning. Now, the word *interpret* has several connotations: to explain, to translate, to construe. All involve making a connection. This is what the teacher does. He puts the student *in connection* with the problem at hand, and leads him to seek and press an engagement with it.

Finally, in the great teacher, no matter how unobtrusively, there will be found strength of conviction. Faulkner in his Nobel Prize speech said of the writer: he must "leave no room in his workshop for anything but old verities and truths. . . . Until he does so . . . he writes not of the heart but of the glands." We might say the same of the teacher. In his role of interpreter, his own heart and convictions will come through—subtly and quietly, perhaps, but they will come through.

We hear much these days about the bleakness of the impersonal university, the neglect of teaching, and the pressures for research and publication. There is ground for concern, along with some exaggeration, in these charges. Let me mention just three of the many reasons why better teaching must be nourished and sustained on our campuses. One is obvious enough: the rapidly growing number of college and university students, which means that there are going to be proportionately fewer competent teachers. Accordingly, the role of those teachers who can, by leadership and contagion, encourage and assist others is ever more crucial.

A second compelling argument for doing everything we can to strengthen and enrich the teaching on our campuses grows out of the exploding diversity of knowledge. Not only in the sciences and social sciences but also in the humanities, marked changes are discernible in the materials being studied and in the approach to these materials—a movement which is on the whole a healthy one towards fundamental analysis and basic principles, away from mere memory work and dependence upon fixed segments of subject matter. But it does call for more talented teachers.

Rote learning never was much good. Today it is worth even less. The citizen of tomorrow must master the ways of analysis and be able to search deeply if he is to cope with the uncertainties and changes of the decades ahead. The kind of education that will equip him to do so cannot be offered by second- and third-rate minds using second- and third-hand methods of instruction.

A third reason for stressing the importance of teaching in higher education today involves its Heraclitean tension with research, and the emphasis and glamor now so widely attached to the latter. Please do not mistake me. The quest for new knowledge is vital in the university, and in the liberal arts college too. On campuses all over the country the stepped-up range and tempo of research have strengthened and enlivened instruction far more widely than they have deadened or disabled it. In the college or university, research and teaching are indeed two ends of the same bow:

neither has much force without the other. That is what the ideal of the teacher-scholar is all about. But at a time when there are not enough good teachers to go around and the supply is falling still farther below the demand, it is of national importance that such good teachers as we do have not be lured away from teaching.

I am concerned here particularly with the drift toward sharply reduced teaching loads in many universities. It seems to me to have gone dangerously far. There is, to be sure, good reason for reducing the teaching duties of men and women with unusual capacities for research or with great gifts as lecturers or writers. It enables such people to bring their talents to bear in the best way. *All* college- or university-level faculty members should have the time to do research, in their chosen fields of study. What I am dubious about is that by-product of today's intense competition for faculty wherein part of the lure is a weekly teaching assignment of no more than a few hours—and sometimes none at all. Whether they mean to or not, institutions which go in heavily for this kind of enticement are making the avoidance of teaching a reward and a mark of status in a way that can only be harmful to higher education.

I do not advocate or defend the overly heavy

teaching load, which is still too often the rule in some types of institutions. It, too, is at odds with good teaching and brings low returns in students' learning. But in many of the leading institutions today the trend is toward the other extreme. So much so that I suspect the day may not be far off when legislators or trustees will be inquiring into the provision of substantial salaries for college and university faculty members on ridiculously low teaching schedules where there is not the exceptional promise or achievement to justify it. Some embarrassing questions may be asked.

In general, though, I believe that the tension between good research and good teaching is a balanced one and will remain so, and that the common sense of America's academic folk will prevail so that good teaching will have its proper place of honor among them. Meanwhile it falls to all of us to help to keep that balance and preserve the dignity of the teacher-scholar as teacher, not solely as scholar. This cannot be the concern of deans and presidents alone, but must be that of departments and individual faculty members as well. It is precisely there that the battle for effective teaching will be fought and won.

WHAT I HAVE SAID of the good teacher makes it clear, I think, that even in this day of spectacular advances in the technology of communication, he is not about to be replaced by television and other mass media, important as those may become in higher education. Insofar as education is conceived of as primarily training—that is, the inculcation of facts, of routines, of memorizable techniques and procedures—it requires of the student little more than passive reception; he need only be the good little pitcher already mentioned. For this, a close relation of learner to teacher has little point; large classes are nearly as effective as small ones; students educated by television sometimes test even higher than those who face a teacher in the flesh.

Training is basic to every field of learning. Yet at almost every level, and certainly at the college and university levels, education must go far beyond that. This means that if we wish to raise up men and women who can exercise independent judgment and responsibility, we must give them an educational experience which is to some significant extent active, not merely receptive; individual, not solely group; living, not canned.

We must not expect too much, then, from techniques of mass instruction. Perhaps in some technical and vocational fields of study, the pressures can be ridden out by greatly enlarged classes and an extensive use of television and mechanical aids. And probably in places where almost all instruction is already done in classes of thirty or more, doubling of class sizes will matter little. However, education of quality in that fundamental range of subjects we commonly designate as "arts and sciences" can never prosper—or even be effective— if it is reduced to a mechanical process of transferring information.

To be vital, to produce genuine thinking and creative habits of mind, education in these fields requires opportunities of give-and-take, in some degree of intimacy between the student as an individual and teachers who themselves exhibit a spirit of inquiry, of rational deliberation, of intellectual creativity, of honest judgment. To be sure, there are always some enterprising students who will go beyond the limitations of narrow training and of mass instruction on their own. But how hazardous it is to leave this to chance! How wasteful to fail to quicken in our best young minds the life that is in them!

In determining the scope and extent of the effort required adequately to staff our colleges and universities, we cannot afford to let lesser objectives crowd this one out of our sights. Indeed, just because mass communication has won such a dominant position in so many areas of our life, we need to work the harder for this more personal objective —living teaching—in our colleges and universities. The creative, thoughtful, mature minds we must develop for college and university teaching, no less than for other important aspects of our national life, are not likely to be mass-produced. Let us work and hope for a much higher degree of far-seeing self-interest among the American people upon this issue.

5

MIND & SPIRIT

A TENSION which seems to me no less important today for its being somewhat out of fashion is that between the university's obligation to deal with the minds of its students and at the same time its obligation to give attention to moral and spiritual values—and not only in its students but in itself as well.

Trained intelligence is a two-edged sword. Directed to mean or violent ends it can vastly extend our capacities for degradation and self-destruction; nor can it insure that we shall always pursue the good even when we perceive it. But just as intelligence when trained extends our destructive capabilities, so does it extend our capabilities for humane and worthy ends.

I think of two men of our century, both trained in European universities, both highly intelligent. The one, Dr. Joseph Goebbels, became Hitler's chief minister of propaganda, the champion of the "master race," the exponent of the glory of war, the architect of the "big lie." The other, Dr. Albert Schweitzer, a symbol of Christian charity, gave to the world not only profound and searching theological scholarship, and brilliant and dedicated musicianship, but a life work of self-sacrificing devotion to healing among primitive peoples.

This ambivalence of the intelligence is deep-set and age-old. Sophocles sought to probe it as a tragic theme nearly two and a half millennia ago. One deceives oneself if one ignores this duality, and it would seem to me one of the functions of a liberal education to learn to recognize it and to face its implications.

We are fearfully and wonderfully made. Willfulness is part of our nature, and no man knows its mystery. To Shakespeare there was no answer but to try to understand and face the tragedy of life with compassion and high purpose: "the readiness is all." To Milton the solution lay in obedience to God, "in whose service is perfect freedom"; but he saw that this also entailed a continuing searching of the mind and the spirit to fathom the unknown things of God's creation, the better to do His will on earth.

One fundamental assumption in the idea of a liberal education is that the informed and enlightened mind has heightened capacities both to know and to work toward the good. For myself, I would not for a moment be a university administrator if I thought that education has nothing to do with moral power, that the opened mind and the trained intelligence were not potent implements both for human self-realization and for human welfare.

To be sure, no one would argue that the calculus, or linguistics, or the laws of thermodynamics teach right conduct. Yet on reflection we know that even the most depersonalized of such studies teaches a respect for truth and, when rightly taught, carries along other virtues that can enlighten our powers of judgment and decision—for example, accuracy, perseverance, honesty, imaginativeness, dispassioned reasoning, curiosity, and humility before the unknown.

Thus the experience of a liberal education, even in its most purely intellectual aspects, has more than a cerebral meaning; and the study of man and of his affairs—through history, philosophy, the arts, or any of the social sciences—inevitably involves one in fundamental issues of human values, issues that relate to oneself. Education is of real use to the person who holds to the respect for truth which animates those who have taught him: respect for truth about our physical world of time and space and material phenomena; respect for truth about the history of men and the forms and dynamics of their social existence; respect for truth about man as a creature, possessing not only cognition but the power of choice, a being plagued not only with inherent willfulness but gifted with a capacity for outgoing love and a deep-set hunger for spiritual fulfillment.

The world has had enough of the fruits of ignorance and of misguided prejudice in human affairs to teach us that thinking and trying to reach a reasoned grasp of principles, as of practicalities, should precede action. And if one doubts that the development of the mind bears a direct relation to the practical problems of the modern world, let him ponder both the scientific and technological requirements posed by national defense in our time, the problems of the "inner city," and—even more fundamentally, I believe—the very idea of a free society.

The concept of the government of a people by themselves presupposes critical intelligence. Especially in this country have we built our house on

the foundation of an electorate and of public serv-
ants informed and able to distinguish the fraudulent and the ill-advised from the genuine and the
long-term good. Here, almost taken for granted in
our political life, is an assumption that informed
thought and purposeful action are linked. And if
the founding fathers were realists enough to build
checks and balances into our constitutional system,
they were so because of intellect and intelligence.
Should it be argued that our society has often
failed to avoid the fraudulent and ill-advised, there
remains but one reply: there is no other recourse,
indeed no way of even assessing our successes and
failures, without informed and enlightened intelligence.

Nor can we, with intelligence, look into human
affairs without realizing that men's aspirations for
significance and value are ever at stake. The mind
of the educated man is properly focused not only
on the mechanics of our social and political existence, critical as these are, but also on the fundamental values which undergird a free society and
make possible the opportunities for self-realization
that he enjoys within it. I mean, for example, belief in a republican form of government, in equality
of opportunity, in intellectual freedom, in the dignity and worth of the individual.

We benefit by these values because generations of ardent and clear-sighted men and women have nourished them and have labored not just blindly to make them part of the working stuff of our social and political existence. And even as one comes to recognize all this, however dispassionately, he must, it seems to me, recognize that without the support of individual effort, diligently and intelligently given, this heritage would wither and these beneficent principles would cease to remain effective forces in our common life.

As I said in the opening paragraphs of this book, it is not my intention to deal here with specific problems of higher education today. But I cannot resist pointing out that our colleges and universities owe one pressing problem, as does society as a whole, to past neglect of a moral responsibility. I refer to the urgent, critical problem of the black student in the university and the black citizen in our society, a problem we face now precisely because for so many years we refused to face it, because we neglected our moral duty to offer a helping hand to the poor and the socially underprivileged. Of course, if a remarkably brilliant poor boy appeared on the scene, the doors were open to him almost everywhere. Or if a young person had extraordinary determination, he could always find ways of putting himself through college, and often professional education as well, even if his family could contribute nothing. But only in recent years has it dawned on us that we could not go on merely serving such exceptional cases; that in doing so we were failing to meet the needs of our society generally, were being unfair to many young people of great, though hidden, potential, and that we were leaving truncated and inadequate the quality of life within the colleges and universities themselves.

As one responsible for a residential university, I feel this last point keenly. Some of the most important growing and learning in college occurs through the mixing and rubbing of students with one another. It is in these associations no less than in the classroom that future leaders test and enlarge and mature their convictions. This means that a fully healthy collegiate or university community will include students from widely varying socio-economic backgrounds, and will seek to extend its services to a wide cross-section of the American society. Otherwise the institution is bound to be out of touch with both the temper and the needs of the American republic as they present themselves to us now, and as they seem sure to present themselves even more demandingly in the years ahead.

These are sure to be difficult years with respect to race relations, the alleviation of poverty, and the restoration of our cities. For these conditions there are no panaceas to make up for decades of indifference and neglect. And education, which offers the best hope for progress in solving these problems—both in long-range terms and day-by-day—is far from being a guarantor of peace and tranquility. For as it quickens the minds and raises aspirations, education does not always generate heightened admiration for what is; nor does it always instill patience with what should not be. Yet only through education can we hope to work through these huge problems of technological unemployment, of decaying urban centers, and of dangerously strained racial relations.

As Gunnar Myrdal has said:

American affluence is heavily mortgaged. America carries a tremendous burden of debt to its poor people. That this debt must be paid is not only the wish of the do-gooders. Not paying it implies a risk for the social order and democracy as we have known it.

One would think that by now most Americans would be aware of the debt we owe and the danger we face. Unhappily, there remains in this country a fearfully widespread blindness to the explosive potential of the inequalities which the blacks still suffer generally within the American society. Most educational institutions are now making great efforts to catch up. If our efforts do not always seem to be fully appreciated—if we are sometimes impatient, frustrated, or disappointed by the response of black youth to the promise of reward through better education—it is important to realize that this promise has been made to them before, by people no less sincere or dedicated than ourselves.

THERE ARE SOME who maintain that education should not pretend to make men better—only better informed, more efficient. I hesitate to attempt to answer the question asked of an earlier teacher in Plato's *Meno*: "Can you tell me, Socrates, if virtue can be taught? If not, is it a product of practice? Or does it accrue to men by nature, or in some other way?"

I do suggest, though, that whatever the answer may be, we as individuals had better give more of our time and of ourselves to thinking about right and wrong in our own little worlds and in the larger world around us. In a university, where we hope that there are fewer axes to be ground, fewer selfish interests than in most other places, we ought to have an atmosphere conducive to such reflection and meditation.

Let me put it another way. I do not know how to teach good conduct, nor how to convert clear thought into right action. There is no set of gears to connect, no button to push, no computer to program to do that. But I do believe that right action is the proper goal of our lives in the here and now, and that clear-eyed intelligence and thoughtful reflection can contribute much to its attainment. As Pericles reminded the Athenians, we can have "a peculiar power of thinking before we act and of acting too." And if we often fail to achieve the goal, let us at least *know* that we have failed.

For a hundred years or so strong currents in western thought have been trying to dehumanize man. Some interpreters of Darwin, of Marx, and of Freud have urged on us a new picture of man, not as a spiritual being but as a kind of advanced animal mechanism. Meanwhile, man himself has become so delighted with the machines of his own creation that he has even begun to imitate them, to imagine he can order his own life mechanistically —as well as the lives of others. Thus we get much talk about adjustment, social engineering, and the planned society; students are described as "products," as though a school were a factory; behavior is justified in terms of average expectancy; and almost nowhere in all this talk do we hear of wisdom, compassion, honor, or nobility.

Now, I do not happen to believe that we are going to build a world much worth living in if we put our faith entirely in mechanistic theories, in calculating machines, in statistical measurements and norms. These things must be our tools, not our idols; valued means, not determiners of our ends.

I believe that man can still have confidence in himself as something more than a conditioned animal mechanism; that he can still have faith in himself as a spiritual being, acknowledging what is holy within himself and beyond himself; that he can give thanks for the gift of reason, for the capacity for compassion, for good and high intent, for the power of choice, for strength of will, for noble actions. *Nobility*, *magnanimity*, *greatness of soul*: These words are not much in the modern idiom, but heaven knows this troubled, perplexed, uncertain world needs them and needs them aplenty.

Let me add, though, that it is very easy to invoke high principles when they serve one's purpose, and to retire them to the dust closet when they get in the way. Educated people especially seem wonderfully able to make matters of self-interest take on cosmic overtones. Disraeli is said to have observed of one of his contemporaries that he didn't so much make his conscience his guide as his accomplice; that is an easy habit for any of us to fall into.

Then there are the extremists who press their absolute demands on grounds of principles. Armed with self-righteousness and simplistic dogmas, they are quick to deny to those who oppose them all claims to veracity or good will. If you disagree, you are a scoundrel. Because your views are contrary to theirs, your every argument is specious, your every motive sinister. May I suggest that ideals are to be cherished and pursued, but the absolute insistence on all or nothing does little to improve things on this troubled planet. Indeed, to demand all or nothing is, more often than not, a psychotic reaction which reflects a distorted sense of reality.

The problem is an old one, and always difficult. We should not compromise principles at our own convenience; nor, on the other hand, can we justifiably demand that our views prevail absolutely. In the face of this dilemma, some prefer to brood alone in the dark or deck themselves with ornaments and withdraw to inner worlds of fantasy. But these are hardly practical options. The question of conduct based on principle is not simple. The answers will not be found once and for all, but must be sought in the grubby, day-by-day business of living and working as honorably as one can, without self-delusion and without despair.

To TODAY'S IDEALISTIC STUDENT I would say that other generations have been restless too, have raised troublesome questions and challenged old attitudes, have known something of idealism and of the sense of being let down, have inherited a free society and tried to make it more free. Whatever good has been accomplished in our time, we have come to recognize that in it there is a large measure of debt to the past.

Robert S. McNamara observed in an address:

All the evidence of history suggests that man is indeed a rational animal—but with a near infinite capacity for folly. History seems largely a halting, but persistent effort to raise his reason above his animality.

He draws blueprints for Utopia. But never quite gets it built. In the end, he plugs away obstinately with the only building materials really ever at hand: his own part-comic, part-tragic, part-cussed but part-glorious nature.

Here briefly summed up is a statement of the inextricable blending of things in human affairs which wise men long have recognized. It is a statement of the validity of both the comic and tragic view of life.

The comic view sees the distortions, the pretensions, and the folly in man's efforts; but it does not despair of man. The tragic view, which is realistic, too, but fed from deeper emotional springs, sees man's strengths and nobility and high promise undercut and brought low by his pride and feebleness. But to abandon hope is not its counsel either. Both views are true; they are complementary. To know them, to make them one's own, can help to keep one sane and steady.

As human creatures we are not fully knowable, even to ourselves. Yet, over the centuries from the Greek philosophers and Hebrew prophets down to the present day our profoundest thinkers have achieved certain insights about human nature. One is that it contains great capacities both for good and for evil. At various times in the history of ideas, the optimistic view of man has prevailed. It did so in certain writers of the Renaissance, in some "men of reason" of the eighteenth century and in the idea of progress which they passed down, in Marx and his dream of a classless society, for example. And some of this radical optimism survives today, both in those who envisage cool scientific utopias and in those others who would confront the harsh complexities of life with such fragile and lovely weapons as flowers. But always men's capacity to go wrong, their selfish and acquisitive instincts, their just plain orneriness, have risen up to refute the romantics. And it would seem to me that they do so in abundance now.

The Greeks had a proverb: χαλεπὰ τὰ καλά —"Things worthy of admiration are never easily won." Perhaps it takes strain and tension and challenge to bring out the best in a people. If this is so, the times into which we have moved may be the saving of us. For it seems abundantly clear now that American peace and prosperity are not isolatable from the rest of the world, and that if we mean to uphold that which we know to be truly admirable in human terms we shall have to make contest for it in a determined and intelligent way both here in this country and around the globe.

Somehow we have to recapture a sense of challenge, a readiness to sacrifice, a willingness to strive hard and take risks for the things that contribute to the humanness of human dignity. One of the most basic of these things is freedom— not freedom as anarchy or as license, but freedom under law and freedom as self-accepted responsibility. There is great generative power in freedom when it is so conceived and loved, and when people recognize that it is not self-perpetuating but ever requires renewal and rededication.

A wonderful passage in the fifth book of Herodotus' history speaks to this point—when he describes the transformation of Athens after it had thrown out its tyrants and set itself up as a democracy (under the reforms of Cleisthenes) toward the end of the sixth century B.C.:

> It is plain enough not only from this instance, but from many anywhere, that freedom is an excellent thing; since even the Athenians, who, while they continued under the rule of tyrants, were not a bit more valiant than any of their neighbors, no sooner shook off the yoke than they became decidedly the first of all. So soon as they got their freedom, each man was eager of himself to do the best that he could.

I have sought to say that in protecting and advancing the institutions of freedom we need to be guided by a realistic, non-utopian, anything but complacent, but nevertheless optimistic view of human nature. The founding fathers of this country were realists in this sense, or else they would not have built so many checks and balances into our instruments of government. But they were idealists, too. They believed—no, they knew!— that mankind's finest expressions and men's true humanity lie in man's unique though limited capacities as a rational and spiritual being, capable of intelligent self-direction and self-government, under the grace of God.

This attitude too, and its implied respect for intellectual and spiritual values, we must recapture. Here those responsible for education, for political leadership, for our churches, for our media of mass communication—indeed, all who are in a position to help influence popular attitudes on a large scale —bear, it seems to me, a particularly urgent responsibility to uphold what is admirable and worthy of us.

The spirit of freedom and its institutions—the intrinsic worth of the person, the higher life of the human mind and spirit—these are not values which are self-securing on a wide popular basis. They require fully as much conscious effort and alert application as does the struggle for material success. In short, the things that most of us inwardly know to be worthy of our love have to be worked for. They are not automatically won or sustained. They seldom, if ever, have been.

E ARLIER I SAID that the university shares with the family and the church responsibility for instilling appreciation of moral and spiritual values in young people. I have no formula for the division of this responsibility, but I am not one of those who believe that higher education ought to be carefully insulated against all religious influence. Indeed, I feel that while religion can sometimes be a dangerous and disruptive force, it is also among the most vital and enriching manifestations of the human spirit. As Rachel Carson feared an over-use of chemicals in *Silent Spring*, I would fear an indiscriminate use of anti-religious DDT lest it wipe out precious and irreplaceable attributes of humanity.

I believe that a religious man must be educated, and an educated man inspired. Either quality by itself is insufficient—like an airplane with a motor and no wings, or wings and no motor. A man needs both reason and faith, and probably never more so than in turbulent and uncertain times like our own.

In an earlier period of controversy, when the new science was first making itself felt, a devout physician, Sir Thomas Browne, wrote in his *Religio Medici*: "I teach my haggard and unreclaimed reason to stoop unto the lure of faith." Certainly in the present day a prime need is for churchmen and educators to work with greater sensitivity, and wherever possible in more effective interaction, to help men find and affirm a positive meaning in life beyond the cults of self-gratification which are so prevalent. Despite the great growth in college enrollments and the swelling of church membership lists in the recent decades, neither American education nor the churches can claim to have adequately recognized and reached the unfulfilled inward needs of millions of the young people whom they touch. There is a void in many of these young lives, where confidence in creeds and moral codes have been eroded by failures in family living, by community indifference, by the rampant materialism all around them, or by tired and dusty preachments at the very time that their minds were being quickened and stretched by schooling.

We live in an age that puts a high premium on trained intelligence, on the uses of intellect, and on reasoned efficiency. American universities have helped to bring about these conditions, and part of the consequence is that the churches are confronted with a need to speak to the members of such a society in terms that relate to these aspects of their educational experience and these demands in their productive lives. To such a people the churches cannot speak simply wishfully, pontifically, or pietistically, and expect to have much impact. They must reach human beings whose eyes have been opened by education, who find in trained intelligence the principal pathway to worldly success, but whose innermost needs are yet unfulfilled.

The sadness of it is that often they are unaware what these needs are—though many able intellects *have* been able to recognize their own spiritual poverty, and sometimes their very doubts and dissatisfaction have helped them find a faith. Paul Elmer More in his *Pages From an Oxford Diary* tells of having moved through both materialism and the opposite view that regards the world as an illusion to quest for "a dynamic, personal agent" at work in our lives. "That made me a better, as well as a more complete, Platonist," he writes, "and it set me again on the road to Christianity.

. . . Why should a man call himself reasonable unless he knows the limits of reason?"

But most of us, including many of our college and university students, do not have the philosophical grasp of a Paul Elmer More. Their university training carries them far along roads of knowledge but does not open for them the wider vistas of faith. They rest uncomfortably in their doubts, never perceiving that skepticism can be something more than a plaintive negativism. It is, at its best, a process through which or by which one hopes to arrive at the truth. It need not be at odds with faith. I recall hearing a preacher declare that every good Christian has in him some skepticism. As Emerson puts it in a famous metaphor, the ground the skeptic occupies may be, for all he knows, the vestibule to the temple.

I have no panaceas, but just as the greatest teachers and preachers have reached men by the power of example, I believe that we in our educational institutions must try to be examples for those who will follow us. And it is fortunate that we produce from time to time men and women who in themselves embody the best of human performance and aspiration and to whom we can point with confidence.

To TALK BRIEFLY of religion is always to risk being misunderstood. To lessen that risk let me say that I believe, as have many wiser than I, that one of the most precious possessions in all this perplexing life is the enlightenment of mind which comes from the habit of seeking and facing the truth, of probing and seeing under the mere surface of things. The religion whose influence I would have in higher education is not one that impedes the search for truth.

One of the oldest bits of human wisdom is that things are not always what they seem. Plato pictured mankind as persons in a cave watching flickering shadows on the wall, shadows which are not the true reality but only suggestive of it. From the Bible we have the wonderful phrase of seeing through a glass darkly. The educated man is never content to take appearances for realities, or to react wishfully when a situation calls for the hard exercise of thought.

In his essay *On Truth*, Francis Bacon once asked, "Doth any man doubt, that if there were taken out of Men's Mindes, Vaine Opinions, Flattering Hopes and the like, but it would leave the Mindes of a number of men poor shrunken things; full of Melancholy, and Indisposition, and unpleasing to themselves?" In his "Digression on Madness" in *The Tale of a Tub*, Jonathan Swift put the matter more ironically, praising "the wisdom that converses on the surface [of things]" because it brings that "sublime and refined point of felicity, called the possession of being well deceived; the serene peaceful state, of being a fool among knaves."

What we find beneath the surface of things is seldom entirely cheering and pleasant. When we look searchingly and consider carefully, we find much that is imperfect, much to shatter our illusions. For some, despair and cynicism may follow. But most of us, if we have courage, would prefer to have such clear sight as we can. We would prefer to know as accurately as possible where we are and in what kind of world. Whatever it be, we wish to see it clearly, and to be able to distinguish the beautiful from the ugly, the good from the bad, the true from the false.

It is on that word "courage" that I would close. Hostile forces anchoring on selfish interests, or the *status quo*, have in every century opposed those institutions dedicated to the advancement of learning and the betterment of human life, and we would be rash indeed to underestimate these forces. Nevertheless, born as it is of our society, the American university must not surrender its role as foregazer and critic—as searching mind and probing conscience—of that society. Perhaps the highest and most difficult function of the university, its most irreplaceable form of service in a free society, lies here: that is, not merely to be an instrument responsive to popular pressures, but, with due temperance born of a long heritage and enduring tradition, to be willing to stand up as a judge of society's tastes and actions. The critic and the judge are not always popular, but the greatest teachers in all ages have preferred hard truth to comfortable fiction and self-respect to popular esteem. Courage, with temperance, is always needed to hold the university to its role and mission: courage on the part of men and women of good will who cherish the spirit of liberal learning and seek a better day for their fellowmen. So girded, the university as a human institution can be confident not only of its past but of its present and future, ready to stand up for its aims and basic commitments, bold to make its voice heard in the land.

Date Due 94616
